T0000928

Dig, Dance, Dive

How Birds Move to Survive

Written by
Etta Kaner

Illustrated by
June Steube

Owlkids Books

Birds
don't just
fly.

They also move in unusual and surprising ways. They dig, dance, dive, dabble, and much more. Wonder how and why birds make their amazing movements? Read on to find out!

Birds
Walk

A pheasant-tailed jacana can swim, but it prefers to walk on water—sort of. Actually, it walks on the leaves that float on the water. Its super-long toes and claws spread out the bird's weight to keep it from sinking. The toes are also handy for lifting the edges of leaves to look for prey hiding underneath.

Birds
Toboggan

What does an Adélie penguin do when it wants to move *fast*? It lies on its belly, pushes with its feet, and toboggans. *Wheeee!* Tobogganing uses less energy than walking. But all that sliding can harm a penguin's feathers. So the Adélie penguin makes sure it smooths and oils its feathers with its beak to keep them in tip-top shape.

Birds Climb

The kakapo can't fly, but it *is* a good climber. It clambers up trees to find food and escape danger. See that hooked beak? The kakapo uses it, along with its strong feet, to hold on to branches as it climbs. How does it get back down? It parachutes by spreading its short wings!

Birds Run

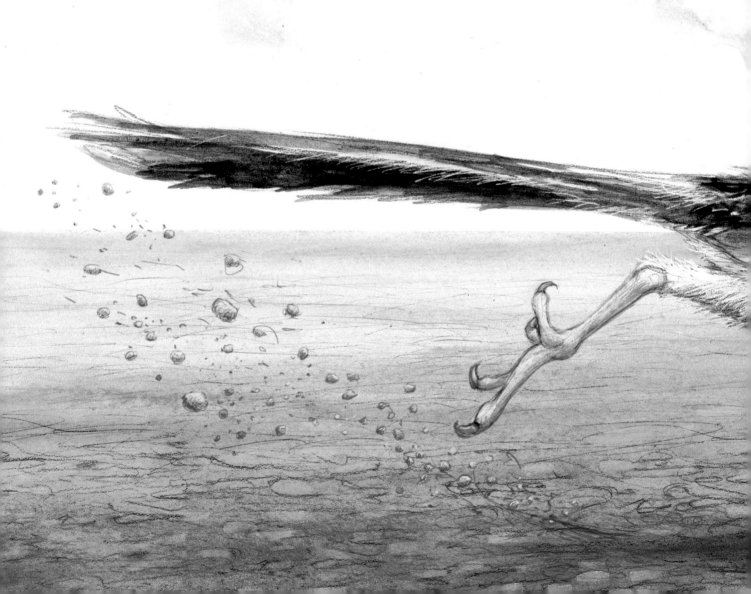

The greater roadrunner may be small, but it can run faster than you!
When hunting, it zips along on its strong legs, using its long, straight tail
for balance. Catching tasty meals of insects, lizards, mice, and even snakes
is a snap for this speedy bird.

Birds
Dig

Imagine digging a giant hole with your feet. That's the first thing a male mallee fowl does when it builds a nest. The hole is as deep as the height of your kitchen counter! Then the hole is filled with a huge pile of leaves and sand in which the female lays her eggs. As the leaves rot, the pile heats up— perfect for keeping their eggs warm!

Birds Dabble

Mallard ducks dabble to find food. They tip head down and tail up in shallow water. *Gulp!* Water, along with floating plants, worms, or insects, enters their mouths. Their bills then act like a strainer. Tiny comb-like teeth along the edges allow water to be pushed out while food stays in.

Birds
Dance

Before a male superb bird of paradise dances to impress a female, it changes its look. It pushes the feathers on the back of its neck forward to create an oval. And it lifts its beak to show off bright blue feathers on its chest and head. Then it's time to dance! The male bounces back and forth, with its colorful front facing the female. Wouldn't *you* be impressed?

Birds *Stalk*

The black egret is one sneaky bird. As it steps through shallow water stalking fish, it tucks down its head and makes an umbrella shape with its wings. This creates a shady spot where fish like to gather. Little do they know that the shade is really a trick the egret uses to catch lunch!

Birds Twist

How far can you twist your neck? Like many owls, a long-eared owl can turn its neck nearly 270 degrees in either direction. That's almost all the way around! Why does it do that? To see better.

An owl can't move its eyeballs because they're not round like yours. They are tube shaped. So instead of moving its eyes, the long-eared owl twists its neck.

A blue-footed booby dives from great heights to catch fish. Its streamlined body enters the water at about 60 miles per hour (100 kilometers per hour). That's as fast as a car on the highway! How does it do that without getting hurt? It has special air sacs in its head to cushion and protect its brain.

Birds
Dive

Birds **Spin**

How fast can you spin? A phalarope spins in lake water up to sixty times in one minute! It does this to catch food. As it turns, it creates a whirlpool. The whirlpool sucks up tiny animals from the muddy bottom to the surface. The phalarope then dips its long bill into the water and snatches its prey. Spin, dip, spin, dip—YUM!

Birds
Jump

Male widowbirds have a jumping contest to attract
a mate. But first, each male grows super-long shiny
tail feathers. Then he cuts down grasses to make a
round jumping stage. Finally, it's showtime. All the males jump waaay
up, over and over again, to show off their long tails above the tall
grass. Each female picks the male she thinks looks best.

Birds
Piggyback

People aren't the only ones who get piggyback rides. Eared grebe chicks
do too! As soon as the chicks hatch, their mom and dad leave the nest with
their young. They take turns carrying the chicks on their backs and hunting
for food. This is a great way for grebe chicks to stay safe from predators and
keep warm under their parents' feathers.

These birds also . . .

Climb

The hoatzin chick has claws on the ends of its wings to help it hold on to branches as it climbs a tree.

Dig

The rainbow bee-eater uses its sharp bill to dig a long underground tunnel for its home. As it digs, it pushes the dirt out with its feet.

Walk

A dipper walks on stream bottoms to hunt for its meals. Special eyelids act like water goggles to protect its eyes and help it see clearly under water.

Run

An ostrich has long legs and can run twice as fast as the fastest human.

Dance

Red-crowned cranes leap into the air and flap their wings when dancing with their mates.

Stalk

The American bittern stalks fish and frogs by hiding among tall reeds that look like the stripes on its body.

Dive

The common loon's solid, heavy bones help it dive deeply to catch fish.

To Joshua, Laura, and Jason Weir, with affection — E.K.

For Jim, with love and gratitude. You make it all possible — J.S.

ACKNOWLEDGEMENTS: A huge thanks to Mark Peck from the Royal Ontario Museum for his time and expertise, to editor Debbie Rogosin for her insight and sense of humor, to June Steube for her incredible illustrations, and to Alisa Baldwin for her creative design. What a team!

Text © 2022 Etta Kaner | Illustrations © 2022 June Steube

All rights reserved. No part of this publication may be reproduced, stored in a retrieval system, or transmitted in any form or by any means, without the prior written permission of Owlkids Books Inc., or in the case of photocopying or other reprographic copying, a license from the Canadian Copyright Licensing Agency (Access Copyright). For an Access Copyright license, visit www.accesscopyright.ca or call toll-free to 1-800-893-5777.

Owlkids Books acknowledges the financial support of the Canada Council for the Arts, the Ontario Arts Council, the Government of Canada through the Canada Book Fund (CBF) and the Government of Ontario through the Ontario Creates Book Initiative for our publishing activities.

Published in Canada by Owlkids Books Inc., 1 Eglinton Avenue East, Toronto, ON M4P 3A1

Published in the US by Owlkids Books Inc., 1700 Fourth Street, Berkeley, CA 94710

Library of Congress Control Number: 2021939051

Library and Archives Canada Cataloguing in Publication

Title: Dig, dance, dive : how birds move to survive / written by Etta Kaner ; illustrated by June Steube.
Names: Kaner, Etta, author. | Steube, June, illustrator.
Identifiers: Canadiana 20210221674 | ISBN 9781771474399 (hardcover)
Subjects: LCSH: Birds—Locomotion—Juvenile literature. | LCSH: Birds—Adaptation—Juvenile literature.
Classification: LCC QL676.2 .K36 2022 | DDC j598—dc23

The artwork in this book was rendered in pencil and watercolor with some digital touch-ups in Photoshop.

Edited by Debbie Rogosin | Designed by Alisa Baldwin

Manufactured in Shenzhen, Guangdong, China, in October 2021, by WKT Co. Ltd.
Job #21CB1625

A   B   C   D   E   F

Publisher of Chirp, Chickadee and OWL
www.owlkidsbooks.com

Owlkids Books is a division of bayard canada